Words Within a Butterfly

WORDS WITHIN A BUTTERFLY

WORDS WITHIN A BUTTERFLY:
UNDER GRACE

JILLYANN MARSHALL

authorHOUSE®

AuthorHouse™
1663 Liberty Drive
Bloomington, IN 47403
www.authorhouse.com
Phone: 1-800-839-8640

Published by AuthorHouse   05/16/2012

ISBN: 978-1-4685-9447-8 (sc)
ISBN: 978-1-4685-9448-5 (hc)
ISBN: 978-1-4685-9449-2 (e)

Library of Congress Control Number: 2012907144

CONTENTS

Chapter One   Trust 1

Chapter Two   Consider My Position......................7

Chapter Three   Not so Elementary Beginnings 11

Chapter Four   You Reap What You Sew.................19

Chapter Five   Seriously? 31

Chapter Six   Out with the Old in with

                        Confusion 39

Chapter Seven   A Journey to Remember.................43

Chapter Eight   An Unnecessary Sacrifice.................51

Chapter Nine   A Brighter Day...............................59

Chapter Ten   Life's Graduation 65

Chapter Eleven   Why Write?....................................71

Chapter Twelve   The Heart of a True Believer 75

Chapter Thirteen   The Truth about Deliverance 83

PREFACE

Between failure and success is work, the possibility of triumphs, a little pain, an amount of struggle that seems minute later, and finally satisfaction. I've come to realize, in my short time on this planet called Earth that if we form a diagram in life, and exclude all those abstract nouns, and overwhelming emotions, and go to the foundation of the failure, we will find the link missing in the bridge that guides us to our God.

When we reach the conclusion that we are failing, we finally grasp that no matter what venue of positive escape we seek, these escapes are all representations of God's grace and mercy. They are his safety net for us. This means that above all God is always the answer.

Proverb 3:4-6

- Trust in the Lord: Even and especially through prophetic and ministerial words of credible others

- With all thine heart: Put all your faith and trust in God

- Lean not to thine own understanding: If that thought does not line up with God, it is flat wrong, we must not linger in thought with any hesitations or reservations

- In all thine ways acknowledge Him: Do not waiver, take things out, or probe information. Don't demean God by giving Him a part of your life, or part of your praise and worship it all belongs to Him.

- He shall direct your path: God has provided us with a plan, a written plan. He's giving us the opportunity to live in abundance here on Earth and the power and authority to speak it into existence. Jeremiah 29:11 Says "For I know the plans I have for you," declares the LORD, "plans to prosper you and not to harm you, plans to give you hope and a future.

When God created us His purpose was for believers to depict His glory on Earth. That is why we are made in His image. Psalm 27:13 says "*I had fainted,* unless I had believed to see the goodness of the LORD in the land of the living. What David meant was that He knew all these great and amazing things that we encounter every day, like the beautiful sun, trees, ocean, even the air we breathe, we wake up every day to the goodness of the Lord in the land of the living. That's awesome.

With all these good things taking precedent, the devil has to come and destroy them, that's his little insufficient job, to corrupt believers and non-believers. God has equipped us with the wisdom, knowledge, and understanding to say no to temptation. After all, our ultimate goal is to be like Jesus.

I believe in method prayer. God gave us instructions, or methods along with a script in order to prevent failure, or the re-occurrence of failure. The thing about becoming a Christian that frightens most people is making a life long commitment to the things of God, vowing one's life to Jesus. The biggest part is trust, the key to any relationship that determines success or failure. If there is a depicted image of the perfect life, with all the money, perfect marriage, friends, careers, before we give our lives to Christ, most people would become a disbeliever all over again when they join the body of Christ. They will come to realize that even with a life in Christ they will still come face to face with temptation. It is up to us to seek and answers, and say no to that temptation.

Life is a word designed for human beings to understand that we are BEING. We do move, we live, and we breathe. It was also designed so that we remember that time is of the essence, and that we do run out of time eventually. Living comes with good and bad, but it is up to us to determine how we will view our individual lives.

The very first book of the Bible discusses the plan that God had for the ultimate creation, life itself. In this strategic, mapped out plan of genius, God envisioned, created, developed, and perfected to art of living, so that we would see His goodness on Earth.

In Habakkuk 2:2 the bible says "write the vision and make it plain upon tables that he, who reads it, may run with it". If it worked for such a project as giving life, then surely we can implement this plan of action in our daily lives. It is amazing to analyze the increments of the Body of

Christ from ages 1 to 100. I've received, wisdom, strength, courage, from every age group. I've been taught by, laughed with, cried with and for all of these people. God built all of us, from the foundation to the trim, with an absolute unchanging purpose. Whether is be through song, dance, speech, writing, anything, He has created us all to exude life.

CHAPTER ONE

Trust

The bottom line is trust. When we serve this all mighty God with the power to soar anyone to their highest of heights, but all the while are in the midst of examples of vessels like I who did not trust God, doubts begin to consume onlookers, spectators, or candidates for Christianity.

Well, thank God He is the God of a second chance. Being under confident or lacking self-esteem causes a lack of trust in one's self. If we cannot commit to trusting ourselves, then how do we expect to place the entirety of our trust in God? Faith actually becomes inquiry, especially if these principles are introduced to a person before they learn what trust is.

I remember there was this engulfing love that God had blessed me with through family and friends and gifts and talents that I refused to embrace. I rejected it time and time again. I had the happiest moments of completion and fulfillment, and then in order to combat the satisfaction I felt, I would rebel or lie. I was not a child who was into doing really bad things, such as drinking or smoking or any drugs, so my only means of rebellion was sneaking or lying about things, that if I had asked my parents, they would have let me do those things. This love and support was so compelling and so pulling, but I would not allow myself, for unknown reasons, to be founded on it.

With not embracing this security, I stood out in the rain of negativity and hatred, but the whole time God protected my life, with this force field of mercy and grace. I was aware that I was being protected. I had thoroughly praying parents. In order to really feel protected or secure, as humans we have to actually associate this with some type of emotion. That is just human nature. But because I could not properly emote this love, I found myself searching for love in improper fashion, especially when it came to friends. That is not God's heart for us.

John 3:16 For God so loved the world (that's us) that He gave His only begotten son, that whosoever believeth in Him shall not perish but have everlasting life.

God wanted us to feel His love so badly that He sacrificed His only son. He even said if we embrace His love and trust and believe Him, that we could live throughout all eternity. Wow, that is some kind of love. Now most new Christians hear this scripture, and after the break down of it are immediately attracted to the most important part, giving. If we pay attention in relationships, a lot of times the only window to true commitment is sacrifice or giving. Something has to be given to symbolize commitment. When I got married June 12, 2010, my husband and I exchanged rings and vows. Those rings are in a circle to symbolize eternal love and commitment, and in the middle of those vows we repeated several different examples of what I like to call "the no matter whats". These are, in sickness and in health, for richer or poorer, forsaking all others etc. Never will there be a relationship that at some point in time will not involve sacrifice. Now with obvious connotation we must sacrifice self and or flesh to please God. Sacrifice is not negative, especially with God, that includes in relationships whether with a spouse, children, or friends. It is the highest form of giving, and each time in some way that relationship will grow.

Sacrifice forms trust. It makes it so apparent to the other person in the relationship that we will always have their back or protect, provide, or take care of them.

I often think about how many sacrifices my own parents made for my sisters and me. Then it occurs to me that all of those things make me who I am today. That love and security that God was developing in me has now evolved into several serving ministries, including Wings of Purpose for people, not much unlike me, who just could not embrace that love and that sense of purpose.

Many things derive from the opportunity to give or sacrifice:

- God gives us a definite depiction of an answered prayer, and suddenly we now see how He manifests His glory.

- Secondly, He maintains the sense of security in Him that will last a lifetime.

- Lastly, He gives us witnessing tool, or testimony to compel others to believe Him as well

I say all of these things with the fact in mind that some people have trust issues that run very deep and are hard to heal, but please remember that nothing is too hard for God. Mark 9:23 says Jesus said unto them "If thou canst believe all things are possible to him who believeth." Again I am a person who dealt with trust issues. I had a time period in my life where I trusted no one. This derived from someone close to me abusing me sexually for years. It consumed me for an unsettling amount of time, but God delivered me out of that very real and truly dark state of mind. Part of my darkness came from thinking it was my fault, because I felt I could not say anything, when in fact God could have saved me from that if I had opened my mouth and trusted Him to handle it. Praise God that it did not result in tragedy, but in victory! I do everything I know God has called me to do in spite of that demeaning and crippling era in my life. Now I stand on the things that God has founded my life on, principles of love, faith, and ministry.

When we trust God, He can break us though any chains and bondage. He can move a mountain, and set us up on a straight and narrow path, but it is up to us to want those things for our lives. Some people want the walls and they want the mountains, just to use them as excuses, again I was one of them, but we absolutely cannot spend our lives drowning in a sea of things ungodly only to go to hell and drown eternally in a lake of fire.

CHAPTER TWO

Consider My Position

I know my life has just begun. I am elated to see the things to come. At this point, I have envisioned where I am going, and honestly I am grateful for even the vision.

I began my life as a vessel for smiles and laughter. It was only two years before I began reading and a week after my third birthday I began writing. From the age of four, I knew there was one thing that I wanted to do for the rest of my life, and that is, write. God gave me a voice, and something to say to encourage people at different points of their lives. I spill my voice onto paper every chance I get. I realized a long time ago that God would not have given me a voice if no one had use for the words of encouragement, His ministry, or my testimony.

Outspoken is an understatement, especially when it comes to a vivid description of who God created me to be, I'm not allowed to shut up. I cannot sit on His words, He won't allow me to. However, people often use that word, outspoken, to describe me. That's okay. I believe if we have an opinion and we opt to share it whenever we choose: we are labeled anything from outspoken to obnoxious, but it is only obnoxious if God did not give us the authority to decree the things that proceed out of our mouths. I have taken the opportunity to embrace the words that He has given me as witnessing tools to the Body of Christ, saved and soon to be saved.

God blessed me with several gifts, and an awesome testimony. He provided me with an abundantly blessed life through prayer, faith, and manifestation. I am a young woman who has been delivered from weight fluctuation, health issues, racism, sexual abuse, and all that these things bring, down to the consumption of depression and thoughts of suicide. I have trouble reminiscing about the victim role, simply because I know dealing with all of this, and overcoming it all, has made me strong. God embedded in me, through all these things, that nothing is bigger than Him, and that all things are possible. I was a child, and even a teenager, with all the love, resources, and credible others that the world could offer, but it took so long for me to embrace GOD's love. I chose not to tell anyone that I was being abused. I never told anybody until my back was against the wall. I sat through these things, I lied, I denied them even to myself, often crying myself to sleep asking God why. Food binges, sickness, mood swings, these all derived from something I could've controlled had I trusted God to do a thing in my life.

I had my reasons. I had a mother who had been through a mirrored situation, and a father who would do anything to protect me and my sisters. I was afraid. I did not trust God to move in my situation, that he could touch my father's heart, or reconcile my family. As a result, this imprisoned me for 8 years of my life. I allowed gluttony, low self-esteem, lies, unappreciation, invisibility, depression, and hopelessness to destroy piece by piece of me until I had nothing else. I did not replenish. I would say that I ran on empty, but that is not true. I filled up. I filled up on lies, lust, and confidence in my figure, and my face. I filled up on vanity. I flaunted my mature body with no intention of doing anything that that would normally lead to. I grew up entirely too fast. I was raised right. I was in church more than most preachers, probably about 4 or 5 days out of the week with my parents and other family members. Both of my parents are Holy

Spirit filled ministers. I had a nice house, we had nice cars, and we had a great relationship, before the enemy tried to consume me with the idea that I was all alone. I became mean when I felt alone. I made everyone in my life pay for every thrust, squeeze, scratch, punch, shove, and derogatory name I was ever subjected to.

At that point no matter how much people spoon fed me the word, I could not find any room to trust God. I blamed Him. I blamed myself mostly. I felt like what kind of a screw up can go through all of this and not cry out. I was killing myself mentally, and that started taking a toll on me physically. Thank God for eventually learning that I am fearfully and wonderfully made by God.

Psalm 139:14

CHAPTER THREE

Not so Elementary Beginnings

I would have to say that the first time I realized that some people truly would not like me no matter what I did was in pre-school, when a peer wanted a toy I had. I went and found her one that was identical, yet she still bit me for the one I had. It taught my toddler mind, immediately, that even if I am kind to a person, they still have a choice whether they want to reciprocate kindness or negativity. It is often funny to me to be reminded of being a baby, where life was full of peace and comfort rather than the adulterous attitude of reality and pain.

By the time I was in the second grade I had even experienced firsthand prejudice. It was driven by a teacher with one black student in a thirty-two student classroom, who could not see herself helping me succeed, because of the color of my skin. I did everything that I could as an eight year old to continue to progress and even excel, even maintaining my honor roll status. I succeeded, but at the end of that term I realized that just because, in my eyes, my mother was the smartest woman in the world, and my father was the strongest man, there would still be some obstacles in my life that I would have to overcome with just me and God. I was not immune to the cruelty and hatred of people. This only jumpstarted the immediate push I had into adulthood, at the ripe old age of eight years old.

· · · · ·

Pattern Poem
1998—Age 8
I am a young girl
Who likes to sing
Who loves to love
Who believes in you & me
Who dreams of helping others
I am divine adolescence . . . .

· · ·

This same year I developed breast, as well as a monthly cycle. I had hips and a figure and I absolutely could not understand why I looked like my mom and aunts, while the other eight year old girls had bodies not much unlike other eight year old BOYS. I was alone for the next two years because my peers thought it was weird to be seen with the girl who looked way older than them. A few times I had to argue with ignorant people about the fact that I was in my correct grade, because they thought I looked that way because I had been held back. To top it all off, at this point some people decided it would amuse or entertain them to abuse my body sexually, for the next 6 years of my life. That was the start of a downward spiral.

On the first day of the fifth grade, I walked into the classroom that belonged to a woman with kind heart and soft spoken words. I could already tell we were not a good match. In this class I became the "cool kid". I developed the ability to call attention to myself at any given opportunity during the day, and it made it very hard for the teacher to keep teaching at all. She couldn't really give us class work, because I would start a conversation with everyone in the classroom if I heard silence, yet I always finished my assignments. Tactlessly, I disrupted her lessons, and made mean comments to people in the classroom. Everyone was noticing a change in my character, so I was disciplined a lot. They just could not pin point where the change in character came from.

Then in an instant, with one question, it all of a sudden did not make me feel good to be mean. When I was asked repeatedly to stop talking in line, after I decided to disregard every request, the teacher finally asked me, "Why do you hate me so much?" I did not even answer, I just stopped talking. I had broken this woman out of revenge to spite people who abused me, yet she wasn't the one hurting me. It had nothing to do with her. For the first time I realized I was disrespectful, obnoxious, and downright mean to people who were there to love, help, and guide me in the right direction.

From the end of that first week of school until Christmas, we had a total of six substitute teachers, after our original teacher quit. I could not help believing that it was my fault, regardless to the countless times that they told us that she was sick. For the first time in a while, I felt something different than physical pain. I now could feel emotion, I could sympathize. I could understand.

That April, I was excited because our yearly test scores had come in and revealed that once again I had received a commended score on the writing portion and passed with high scores on the other parts. I had led over ten solos in the children's choir at my church. My parents were proud of my sisters and me. I had become an exemplary student with great grades again. People could feel the joy of the Lord in my life, even if I *WAS* being molested. That's the goodness about God. He says let the joy of the Lord be your strength Nehemiah 8:10, and that works as long as we maintain that joy. I was letting God's light shine in me, and being obedient, and as a ten year old that is basically our assignment at that age.

My life was going smoothly, as far as I could control, and then one day my private life came face to face with the public. In the middle of music class, during the viewing of one of my all-time favorite musicals, a boy sitting directly to the right of me reached under my shirt and grabbed my breast. I immediately punched him in his noise and kicked him in the groin. I just sat there in a state of shock repeating, "Oh my God!" I literally could not breathe. It was overwhelming. I was not really in that moment, because I was so afraid of people finding out that this happened to me often, and this incident was small in stature compared to the abuse I encountered regularly. I could not do anything but cry until one of my friends stated that he saw the incident, and he would help me tell the teacher and the principal. Thank God for him. He talked to them while I came dangerously close to hyperventilation.

In the principal's office, I could not help but think how much trouble I would be in for fighting. The thought suddenly occurred that my parents might ask if this had occurred before. I tried vigorously to come up with a good facial expression for when I say, "No this is the first time." I had been dealing with this for two years. What would I say, and I know these people were abusing me, but I did not want anyone to die, and I would not be able to take my mother's resentment for my father going to prison for defending me. I was so confused.

When my parents walked into the office, my mama hugged me, and my daddy immediately asked what happened. I told him exactly what happened. Including that I hit him. He replied "you had better hit him". Then he walked away to cool off before his anger took over. While he paced my mother tried to comfort me. She asked me directly if anything like this had ever happened to me before. I assured her that this was the very first time. It hurt to lie to her, but I could not bear the resentment or the condemnation, which I felt, my family would undergo if I told them the truth.

What I thought I had gained from all of that was the ability to fight the molesters. I did not realize that the boy from school left me alone because he was caught by authority, and was in trouble. I figured I would fight them and they would leave me alone, just like the little boy. However, they were older than me and bigger. Not realizing that, is precisely what put me in a very dangerous situation.

One Sunday afternoon I sat on swing by myself in a place where I was normally very comfortable. I was day dreaming about becoming a famous singer and writer. I was not at all paying attention to the fact that my normal group of peers that played with me had left the area. Across the field from me were a group of young men that I should have been secure and safe around, yet at the time I had no idea how unsafe I actually was. As I sat oblivious to the fact that two of the young men had just approached me, I suddenly felt a hand on the back of my neck. I turned around quickly, and from the other direction another hand flew up my dress. I felt fingers the size of a grown man's penetrate my ten year old female parts. I fought and yelled, but to onlookers it would appear that I was being tickled, if anyone heard me across this field at all. When they were satisfied, after squeezing my breast, scratching my legs and punching me to stop the yelling, they went back to the other young men across the field.

I walked into the house with a bleeding leg. I was punished that day for playing rough in a dress. That is the lie I told to avoid anyone finding out what actually happened. I received a band aid, which in no way healed the hurt that I experienced that day. That officially became the worse day of my life.

CHAPTER FOUR

You Reap What You Sew

Middle school was a blur of confusion and ups and downs for me. I won several awards for singing and a few academic achievements, but other than that it really taught me that anyone could be dealing with sexual abuse and their loved ones may never know. I came to that conclusion because I saw girls being groped, squeezed, hit, and misused every day, and no one said anything. My eighth grade year was awesome I was starting to come into my own, but just as soon as we started the school year, my grandfather, Robert Lee Lumpford Sr., passed away after he spent two weeks in the hospital as a result of a stroke. It was very much unexpected. He never had a health issue before. It was devastating to me. I was very close to him. To this day I take pride and use the nickname he gave me, Butterfly, to convey a message of purpose in my ministry. That school year ended with great memories, and sad losses.

. . . . . .

Butterfly: The Loss of My Pa—Pa

2003—Age 13

Butterfly, that's me.
It took a while to understand . . .
How this could happen to me

He always gave all he had.
Even then . . .
You could tell he was glad.

But glad to let him go . . . .
That's an emotion I may never know.

We said we were ok . . .
Lord knows I was lying that day.

My father tried, but that was his father . . .
His hero he finally broke and cried . . .

My tears I tried to hide
So much pride . . . .
Pride failed that day.

The tears kept coming.
An unfamiliar burning went on in me
Rage, Fury.

Something held back from hurting some one
For what had been done . . . .

He called me Butterfly
Until the day he died
I felt that like a lighter and gasoline collide

I should have been nicer
I should have cared MORE
I could have opened that door . . .

I could have helped . . . .
Except
I did not know . . .
He called me Butterfly though.

As I write this

I wont fight this
Despite this . . . . .
I am BUTTERFLY

I'll see him again.

More than a caregiver . . .
Forever my friend.

A love so unchangeable
Helped me to be able
To FEEL enough to cry
And try not to hide
What I felt inside . . . .

I'll never stop being Your
Butterfly.

. . . . . .

When school let out, I attended a teen conference called
Spiritual Encounter, with the youth group of Faith Christian
Center Church. The first night the anointing was so strong,
that God compelled me to completely yield myself to Him
through worship. I lifted my hands and began praising and

thanking and crying out to God for bringing me through sexual abuse, and loss of identity, and suicidal thoughts, and depression. I was so grateful to Him that I had come out of that situation alive and well. I was amazed at the love and fulfillment that I felt after the service was over. As soon as I committed to God, the devil decided to work over time to tempt me back into the mindset of being worthless and ruined.

The ninth grade came and went. I talked to some unimportant people. I was just having fun for once. I upheld my commitment to God, that I would remain a virgin, but no one could tell. The confidence that I'd gained in the end of my term as a middle school student suddenly went from conceited to downright obnoxious. I was very aware of my hips, breasts, small waist, and beautiful face. People told me all the time how gorgeous I was. I was told by several teachers, that year, that I wouldn't always be able to use charm and wit to get by. At the time, even as a very intelligent person, I still didn't believe what they were telling me. I wore very low rise jeans, where you could see my under wear. I wore low cut tops, for an eye full of cleavage, with miniskirts, stiletto heels, and a HORRIBLE attitude. I had no idea I was setting myself up for failure.

For the first time I realized the concept of "what goes around comes around". I had chosen my victims. Guys, teachers, sweet little girls who I felt I could manipulate into hanging on to every word I said. It finally caught up to me when I was disrespectful to the wrong student teacher. I failed to dress out for PE class repeatedly, and was finally sent to the office by a student teacher who was 21. She handed me the referral. When I had begun to walk off, she yelled at me to let me know that I wasn't moving fast enough for her. Instant fury ignited. Immediately following, she shoved me, hard, and without the realization of who I was in an altercation with I quickly swung. I was in shock for a few seconds. I had hit a teacher. We didn't fight. I did apologize. I was suspended, and she was written up for pushing a student.

Later that year I lied on a principal, who just happened to be a close friend of my family. He was very patient, and I was only sent to SAC for three days. A week later a guy who'd known me my whole life lied and said that I had performed oral sex on him on campus. What an idiot. Because of the type of person he was, everyone knew he was lying, but to me, this was just another situation I was in for the year, and to top it all off the next week one of his friends tried to rape me when I told him that I was not ready to have sex.

Truthfully, I should not even have been at the location with him, but that still did not give him the right to neglect that I told him no.

You reap what you sew. It is what it is, sadly. I always thought of myself as the solo type. People flocked to me. But I didn't have a set few. Even when other people tried to make a group of girls I hung out with a clique, it was false, because I had a different type of relationship with each friend, rather than a collective one for the entire group. Freshman year I did not go to the school that my magnet school fed into. I went to the high school that held every race creed religion and color of people. With 2,000, students at a time, West Brook High was the first choice for a safe education, but the last choice for individual attention. I only hung out with a very intelligent and driven group of young women. I had random friends from different groups and backgrounds. I wasn't even concerned about being a part of a group until it actually happened.

When school let out for the summer, the teens of FCCC went back to Spiritual Encounter. When I came back, suddenly, I was best friends with some really nice, truly driven, and very well-known kids. Most of us had parents who were active in the community is some form or another, and we could easily be spotted and picked out in a crowd full of our peers. I had the time of my life. They all did their parts to help me deal with the things I was going through, whether they knew it or not.

Sophomore year was supposed to be the easiest. I was fifteen with not a care in the world. I was still casually talking to my share of guys in order to stay clear of boredom and amuse myself from time to time. Because of my ambition, I took on more and more activities just to say that I was completely filling out my options. I took part in journalism, student council, and Future Community Career Leaders of America. I wanted to be a part of everything I possibly could. I met new people, and all in the first month of school I had adapted to all these things and changes I would deal with through the rest of the year. I had set myself up for easy street.

In October of 2005, hurricane Rita ran through my home town, Beaumont, Texas. My house was destroyed. The drive was horrible for evacuation. It took 30 hours to get to a five hour destination. My family and I moved around to various locations until we were finally able to go back to our house to view the damage.

On October 20, 2005 I wrote a journal entry called A Personal Testimony about viewing my demolished home for the first time. It read:

My crying was done out of dumbfounded devastation. I never had an opportunity to look for joy in the hell bound chaos our government has nicknamed a hurricane. From the very beginning I was told the severity of the situation and did not want to hear it. In the midst of all my losses lies my resting place. What is to be done when you have nothing left? What object can compensate for a legacy you have worked so hard to build through your life's achievements and goals as well pursued? Rita stole my security.

As I write these words I am standing in the dark hole in which I used to lay my every burden down. I used these walls to bottle up every secret I've ever held. And now I feel as if my secrets are without joy . . . life. Our journey to evacuate started as a faith gripped expectation to be back, safe at home within three or four days, after a mini vacation. Well this became anything but a vacation. I just knew it was another false alarm, so I went along with the panic attack that everyone but I seemed to be having. In the total of thirty hours it took my family to reach a destination that was nothing like the bubble I've lived in for fifteen and a half years, real rest was unrealistic. When I finally realized the danger of our situation, my stomach became weak. I tremble at the reminder of living below the prosperity status my daddy worked hard to create for us. I was spoiled, offended to have to sleep on the floor of a shelter with homeless and needy people, but for that horrifying week I, myself, was homeless and needy. I was in that same situation, in the middle of the storm with no way out but in. So there I slept on concrete floor with a rainbow of people just like me. This situation taught me that no matter how much money you have sometimes it just cannot be the answer.

For the first time in my life I saw the truth in my family. My mother is the heart that everyone depends on. My father is protector and provider. My sisters are our reality, and no matter how much I hurt for my lost possessions, I am the optimist. Together we have our own culture. There is none other like us, I could not have survived this without the love and prayers of my family. For about two weeks we slept in a home filled with furnishings not organized by my mom and appliances not put together by my daddy. As if that wasn't displacement enough, we stayed in a three bedroom home with no beds and twenty one other members of my family their guests included. I'd never dealt with something so hard in my life. Of course there was conflict. Especially since our way of life was so different, but despite all we go through we know we love each other more than anything.

In our final stop I actually got to see the reality of the final image of my life in this house,. I cried. I could do nothing more than cry. All my childhood memories lay in a pile of insulation and debris at my feet, and somehow that's alright with me. I appreciate my new beginning, and I love my life as a child of God. I have a new found sanity. You know in spite of all that has happened to me, I am still thanking God daily, because I am so blessed just to be here to see my home. My only hurt is for the people who have nothing to lean on. Everywhere we turn you see one more person in tears just because of change, but we have to grasp positivity. We have to seek love in new things. My quest taught me a new patience and an abundance of hope and built an increase in my faith. I would not change the path of that on coming storm, because it showed me myself.

In conclusion, my journey is not over, and I am glad I had to go through that to get to my next wealthy place. I can only pray that others got the same spiritual assurance out of this that I did. In this paper I have, for the very first time, told my whole story about the loss of my genuine comfort zone, but I've found it in my best friend. In Him also dwells my heart, and I devote all of my security to Him instead of any four walls for the rest of my life.

I was a fifteen year old who had dealt with more than some grown women with families of their own. I had none of my possessions. The funniest thing about this was that I was able to preserve all of my written work and creativity. God spared what mattered. That's why I didn't care about losing material things. He spared my life in more ways than one. I felt like no one could relate to me on a level where they could understand the things that I had been through. I started to strive for a new goal. That was to avoid crying at all costs. If I saw something that would bring me to tears or even close to tears I left the room and didn't allow anyone to see my tears. In turn, for years people have said I had No emotions. I never argued with them. I wasn't even sure, in my own mind, that what they were saying was untrue.

CHAPTER FIVE

Seriously?

I went school with the mindset that I'm going to be myself this time no matter what. The rumors still occurred, but I set that foundation without knowing. Maturity started to set in and I accepted my consequences. I held my head high any way for a while. I had a different personality and different goals than most of my peers. I never gave myself limits. The only thing that often held me back was the fear of failure. That only lasted until my daddy said, "You control satan, and what he can do with the power in your words." That always stuck. I later found a scripture that I live by, James 4:7 resist the devil and he shall flee. If it is in the Bible, then it is true.

I had a best friend this year. More than anything, the assumption was that we had the same goals and views on life and God. When God leaves the picture, so does the friendship. Drama did it. It was over too soon, but at least I know the difference between people who were there for a season and lifelong friendships. Before the fall out it just set my mind at ease to know I had an earthly being to talk to that would at least try to understand me. To lose that is painful.

This was the year that I had fallen in love for the first time and last time, with my heart, Derrick. I told a few of my close friends that I had feelings for a guy who didn't exactly match me . . . . It's funny how God will change you, when you think all the while that you're the perfect one. Now I sat in geometry super confused. Math was never my strong subject. I sat directly in front of Derrick, my crush at the time, and directly to the left of, Cayla, my other best friend. I shared my inner most thoughts through writing with her. She was a realist. I conquered a lot of situations with the help of her prayers. She wanted the same things as me, we were both going to be writers and public speakers. Between my two best friends and a really close friend, we formed a small clique that we named, the Holy Ghost Girl Clique. One friend was the type of person who could stress constantly, that she didn't care what people said about her, but nothing could be more untrue. The things I watched her go through concerning sex helped me stay far away from it for a while. I learned the reality of not following and yielding completely to God would get you hurt as a young teen girl, and I'd been through ENOUGH.

December of this year I attended her party with my cousin and a guy I liked. I had invited Derrick, because I wanted to ask him where he stood with us. I know that that sounds less than intelligent to ride to a party with another guy I liked, but oddly that didn't seem like a big deal to me at the time. Actually, being that I went to three middle schools, I had friends at every high school. Before Derrick, I just thought that talking to multiple guys would never catch up with me, because it was never two at one school. D (as I call Derrick) was a different breed. He actually had goals and morals, despite what people thought of him. In other words, he wasn't having that. I invited him, because I liked him. I paid attention to his every move, until two of my friends got into an argument over a boy, and I had to play mediator. When I finally realized Derrick was missing, I asked around. Josh told me he had seen him leave. I walked outside. He was sitting there on the phone. With no tact, care, or consideration for who he was on the phone with, I immediately started talking to him.

"Hey", I said with a smirk.

"What's up? You good?" He asked, looking like he didn't understand why I was out there with him.

I said "Yea, but I do need to talk to you".

He said "Cool" in the same careless way he always says it.

I began rambling "Well we've been eating lunch together, and you've been carrying my books. I talk to you more than the guys I am dating. (Not realizing how bad that sounded), and I noticed you are always with me even though you have a girlfriend. So where are you with me and you?"

Blunt. I thought I was declaring to him that I was dumping all these guys so I can be with my one true love. That is not what he got out of my attempt. This is what he heard.

"I clearly play around with these guys until I find something new or better."

He replied "Well . . . we're cool, I like you a lot. Honestly you are just about the most real girl I know. You understand me and I love it, but like you said I have a girl, and your boyfriend would not be feeling this at all."

A long pause floated up to the surface of this mess. I stepped back for a second a little bit confused then I said "Yea I thought so".

I kept getting the same question. "Jill, what's wrong?" in so many different forms. People who ask the same question over and over again are even more annoying right after someone hands you your own crushed heart. The worst of this was that my boyfriend at the time was a "school only relationship", poor thing, I didn't even like him enough to be concerned with getting to know him, and I definitely was not bringing him to my parents.

Derrick's girlfriend was unknown. I shouldn't have assumed that my popularity would make me more attractive, and the real me at the time was ridiculous, downright cocky. I had this back and forth image with my peers. Either I was beautiful and generous, or horrible and hateful. Next step bipolar . . . . I don't know. They just had their stigmas. Oddly enough the one thing I wasn't supposed to do was like Derrick Marshall. We were different. People thought my family was rich and that I was some brat who dwelled on materialism . . . . Not true. They thought he was a ghetto thug with no intelligence, sense, or morals . . . Not true.

I was so private that nobody ever knew whether I was in a relationship or not. I kept things to myself, because people looked at a fifteen year old with the body of a 25 year old and made their accusations based on my measurements. Indeed ignorant. I was doing absolutely nothing to be accused of things like that. I didn't even kiss a boy until I was sixteen.

Derrick dealt with a lot of the same things, but on a different level. I had a foundation, and knew I didn't want to stray too far from it. He needed to know somebody cared. I had made up my mind that nobody but God cared and that my parents cared by default. I was completely misguided.

Even though this boy denied me access to his heart, he couldn't deny the God in me. He needed that love. God used me in his life. I was willing to be obedient for something for once, and God used that up. I prayed for Derrick I ministered to him. I went out of my way to let him know that God loved him even if he wouldn't let me. Without the bling, chains, and grills, he was everything I was praying to God for. He promised me the desires of my heart and D surely was that.

Two months after we had our deep conversations, his frequent church visits, and other things, I had my sixteenth birthday party, in the party area at Cheddar's with about forty of my loved ones. That same weekend my daddy gave me his Ford Explorer. I had transportation, great friends, an amazing new start, and another chance to avoid messing up. With all my focus on my good time I didn't realize I had invited "the problem" to the party. I asked Derrick to be my date, I invited a guy I'd been talking to, plus the boy I had just broken up with, because I was pushed into dating him.

My cousin Josh told me one of his friends wanted to date me, and trusting my cousin's judgment I went along with a voice over the phone that seemed to be coming from a very attractive person. The tension that would rise at my party derived from yet another not so proud moment in my book. I agreed to date this guy on the grounds that it didn't get serious. I didn't need the drama at the time. I started seeing this guy, and before I knew it I was talking to another one of Josh's friends on the phone again, and being that they were close friends I should've known this would get hectic.

On one of our group's many Sunday gatherings I got a little too friendly with the other friend, and somehow it got back to the guy I was dating. He was completely hurt. I thought for sure that I wouldn't have to break up with him, because now he had the ultimate reason to break up with me. I had feelings for his friend. However, this only fueled, or ignited his love for me, I guess. He called me nonstop, and then wrote me a message on the popular social networking site, tagged. The message basically said that even though it had only been two weeks he didn't want to be without me. I made my little sister write him a message replying to, what we still refer to as, "the cry for help". She solved it better than I ever could have. Thank you, Jaylann. It was over then, and oddly enough he still showed up to my party . . . . I was in shock. They were all civil. But because of all the drama, I was made out to be the player again, when it really was not like that at all. They were all still my friends. I just wanted them to be at my party. Even though I didn't want to hurt the guy's feelings, I ended up doing it anyway.

All in all my sweet sixteen was still fun, and believe it or not, no real issues derived from the happenings at the party.

CHAPTER SIX

Out with the Old in with Confusion

For a while, over the next month, Derrick and I would talk on the phone a few times. I'd gotten closer to him, and we were both single for about three months. I thought it was amazing to have a male to talk to that didn't want anything sexual from me.

All was well for a few weeks. I had joined the adult praise team at church. I had gotten to another level in my worship realizing nothing was better than being in the presence of God. This was also something me and Keisha, my God sister, and I did together, so I was totally game. God was using me to promote abstinence in several churches and talk to young girls about preserving their virginity. I let Derrick know that I was a virgin and planned to be until I got married. He actually didn't believe me at first, because of the rumors and lies that little boys told to boost their own egos, not caring what they were doing to my name, but I didn't retaliate because I made that bed with my attitude and clothing and mouth. I got so accustomed to him carrying my books, wearing his jacket, him hanging with my friends, and just being comforted by him that I often forgot he still wasn't my boyfriend. It didn't even matter if we had a title. I had prayed for what I wanted, and he was it. I must admit it was more of a guilty pleasure to be attracted to a guy that no one expected me to be with. God showed me he was destined for greatness, and I believed in him. People often judged him based on his anger, violence, and constant tension. When you don't understand your past, and you're unsure of the future, then your present isn't going to look so good. This is a young man who constantly tried to just plain old be the best Derrick he could be continuing to let go of the insecurities of what people told him he couldn't do. He always came out on top even with not much of a solid foundation. He helped me grow as a person and just care for people in general.

March 29, 2006 will be etched in my heart forever. That was the day that West Brook High School soccer team lost two players forever. While I was driving home from the store listening to UGK's Swang, the charter bus housing our traveling soccer team was flipping off the highway ejecting a good friend of mine from the window and rolling onto her red haired beautifully created life and ending it. She was killed. I was at church that Wednesday night when I even found out that there had been an accident. They hadn't released any names, but still I wept. I cried for the pain of a mother having to identify the body of her dead child. An accident is an occurrence in which you cannot place blame on a specific party. It was a bus accident. It hurt. I went home after having Keisha rub my back out of condolence. I sat on the couch like a zombie in front of the news awaiting news I wasn't ready for. "God cover Afton, Colleen, Ashley, Sarah . . . ." I knew them. I had known them since the first grade. No matter which one it would've been I would have been heartbroken because one of my friends wasn't living anymore. I wanted God to keep their lives.

When I found out it was Ashley Brown, I asked God why for months. The return to school was hard. To see all of my elementary school friends mourning over the loss of our friend, who out of all of the mean and hateful people in the world had a one in a million beautiful spirit and amazing heart and an outstanding mind. The other young lady who was killed was Alicia Bonura she was just as loved as Ashley, her parents later started a scholarship fund in her honor. That situation brought pain, then gratefulness, then a new understanding of my own purpose to glorify God while I have a chance. Derrick consoled me through that. He made it clear that I could depend on him, even if he knew I didn't need him to. I was just glad to know he actually cared.

The rest of that school year came and went, and before I knew it, I was working my first summer job.

CHAPTER SEVEN

A Journey to Remember

I spent the first part of summer 2006 working, and spending my money on stupidity, and some guy I was chasing. June was fun for me. I had a good time. I was working I was relaxing and absolutely enjoying my abuse free, stress free, drama free summer. That was a great summer. Then in July my wait was over. One eventful Sunday evening Joshua, Keisha, and Emmett, a good friend of ours, were all over at my house eating my mommy's homemade burgers, playing video games, and making mixed cds. At some point Kei and I got away from the guys, and started talking about some of the guys we were talking to. She had a mission to find me a serious relationship.

When the subject of my birthday party came up, she asked "How's Derrick? Where has he been?"

I replied "I guess he's cool. I haven't talked to him since school let out really."

She said "Right . . . So why don't you call him now", wide eyed, as if she hadn't thought about that until now.

I said "Why? What do mean call him? For what?"

She said, "Never mind Jillyann."

I stupidly thought that was the end of her massive plan for a match literally made in Heaven.

I went in the kitchen to get a cheeseburger, they weren't quite ready yet. When I returned to the living room, she was on the phone with Derrick telling him to come to MY house. At this point I'm attacking her to get my phone! She dodged my attempts and laughed her cackling laugh. That laugh is the one thing that can turn a horrible situation into the best day sometimes. At the time it was worrying me though. When she finally hung up the phone my mouth dropped.

Slowly, I said "What . . . Did . . . . You . . . . Do?"

She replied slyly "I, just hooked you up girl."

I didn't have a response I just waited nervously. I was so glad I had already introduced him to my parents. I wasn't worried about his appearance, because he often cleaned up his act in order to portray a parent friendly version of his school persona. The funny thing is the parent friendly version is who he actually is.

When he got to my house, the doorbell rung twice, before Keisha pushed me to open it. He hugged me. I said "What's up?"

He laughed and replied "Nothing.

I lugged behind him while he walked toward the kitchen, like I often still do, wondering why I said that. He knows I don't talk like that. That's why he laughed at me. He immediately hugged my mama and shook my daddy's hand. I could not believe he was in my house. We laughed, we watched television, and we ate.

He was having fun. The amazing thing about our connection was that the first conversation we had before he asked me to be his girlfriend, was about our futures. After we agreed on everything, he was very straight forward.

"Do you want a relationship with me, a real one?" Those were his exact words.

I replied "yes."

That was that. As the next week went by we tried to see each other as much as possible. He called my daddy to ask for a date. My dad said yes.

That Friday he picked me up from my house. Pause . . . His mother drove him to pick me up from my house. Derrick did not have a car and even though I did, my parents believed in a guy coming to pick me up. He also didn't have his driver's license. Everywhere we went his mom, Mrs. Penny drove us. I can recall his dad, Mr. Tony driving us on one date. That was fun. It was never a dull moment. Oddly enough, I constantly defied my parents about the rules of my car. I drove boys and picked them up. I always had someone in my car, and I constantly skipped school. I was always punished once they found out, though. Confusion is how the devil works, other peoples rules seemed to look better at the time. A number of things could've happened to me. I could've gotten in car accident killing myself, or someone's child who shouldn't have been in my car. I could've been kidnapped or raped outside of school and no one would find me, because they were under the impression that I was at school. As a teenager you never think about the consequences that could possibly come up and greet you from just one bad decision.

On our date, I wore a hello kitty t-shirt and jeans. It was my first official date. He was the perfect gentleman. He came into the house and waited for me to finish getting ready. We'd known each other for two years now, and even with a history this night was new to us. We had never been on an actual date. I fought with others to prove that he wasn't a jerk or thug, yet I, myself, was shocked to find that he knew very well how to open doors and pull out chairs. He even refrained from using the language he used with his friends around me.

Honestly people didn't get us. It was hard to understand. The princess/ b-word, who gets everything she wants, and is stuck up and rude, and doesn't care about anybody but herself, that was me to the public eye. They had summed me up. They called me "rich" girl, whore, the "so-called" Christian. That was the negative point of view.

The people that loved me and were in awe of the things God had done in me, had a dramatically different opinion. To them, I was the blessed one, funny, intelligent, a good friend, generous, DEEP, outspoken, ETC. All these titles I preferred.

Derrick was different. He is not complicated or complex at all. He is what he is. There will never be a time that someone won't be able to read him. Even if he's smiling his biggest smile, you can still see his crying eyes if something is really wrong with him.

The date was nice. I'll remember it forever. We saw the 7:15 showing of Fast and the Furious: Tokyo Drift. I wanted to see Bow Wow in a movie with a bunch of Japanese kids. I was too nervous to enjoy it, though. We held hands. He even kissed me for the first time. Although it was my first date I felt like it was long overdue. I wanted to kiss him for a long time, but honestly I had talked to several guys to say I never had a real kiss before. I was not an affectionate person. I never got close enough to a guy to even think of becoming intimate. It wasn't real, and there was no use pretending.

Derrick's kiss was different; I had never experienced feelings like that before.

I thought to myself "Wow so this is how it feels . . . ."

At that time in my life I didn't feel any pain. If I fell I got over it. There were still no tears. I was sure I had cried all my tears. I thought I was invincible, like a super hero maybe. I couldn't feel anything harmful to me. I had been through so much that I felt it would be purposeless to let anyone else come up from behind and knock me off my joy ride. I did things out of spite to anyone who I thought had ever hurt me. My mother and I stopped talking because I realized we both had breasts, and was stupid enough to think that that made me equal to her. After attempt number 4 of threatening to leave my parents' house, I just stopped.

I stopped everything. Everything I did at school, church, with my family, I simply cut everyone off except for Derrick. I wrote daily and talked to Derrick. No Bible, no prayer, I did nothing. I believe at one point I went about nine months without praying. I was mad at God for all the things I should've purged my heart from so long ago.

CHAPTER EIGHT

An Unnecessary Sacrifice

Almost two months after Derrick and I decided to actually start dating, we were on the phone in deep conversation. I had a day where I made everything I dealt with bigger than God. One of my molesters had come into town, and I had to pretend I cared about one of his many accomplishments. It hurt. I tried to keep it held in, but I broke. I cried right in front of several family members, and I told them it was because I had a bad migraine. I drove myself home, and as soon as I laid down D called me. We talked for about an hour before I randomly told him that I wanted him to be my first and only sexual partner. There was a long pause before he replied.

"Really?" he asked.

"Yes", I said.

He asked why. I made up some crap. The real reason was that I thought since I couldn't give him any of my other firsts, because they were taken from me, that I'd give him the only first time that was worth anything, or at least that's what it seemed like. I thought that would solve my problems.

Being a sixteen year old baby, I had no idea what I was getting myself into. Needless to say, I lost my virginity in September of 2006 at Derrick's house while his parents were out of town. I told my parents I was going to paint signs at a meeting for one of the clubs I was in about an hour and a half before the school bell would ring.

As I approached his house, all of my Godly morals and beliefs came to greet me, yet I arrived and still made the mistake. When it was all over, I had never felt worse in my life. What's worse was that even being molested I didn't give it up, they had to take it. It was wrong. I went against everything I believed in, everything I was an activist for. I walked through the halls of my school feeling like everybody knew as if I wore a sign that was only invisible to me.

I told a close friend, she literally cried. I was proud of my virginity. I spoke in public to girls, groups at a time, and I had failed them all. Never telling them my real story was not wise. I paid for it in more ways than one. I couldn't give myself an answer as to why. I went home and cried. I didn't eat. My clothes looked different. I lost all confidence. I looked more like someone who had committed murder, than a teenage girl who had sex outside of marriage. I had no energy. Nobody could convince me that I would be okay. While I shared true emotions with my friends, I was rude to my mother, and passive with my father, which was a dead giveaway. I have always been a true daddy's girl so to avoid him quickly brought my deeply penetrating pain and guilt to the surface. I continued for a short period of time doing sexual things with D at two of his friends' houses.

One of these times after making a deal with Calvin, Derrick's cousin, that involved us staying at his house while he drove to one of his girlfriend's houses, I got destroyed.

That day Derrick and I made arrangements with Calvin, so that we could go to his house for privacy, rather than the other friend who we couldn't trust to leave us alone. In order to let us take such a risk in his mother's home, he needed something in return. I ignorantly let him take my daddy's truck to visit his friend. While I was in the bathroom trying to muster up to nerve to have sex for the third time, Calvin was driving up to his girlfriend's house directly across the street from my mom's cousin. The greatest thing about this little situation was that this wasn't a long distant relative we barely talked to. My mom did her hair every Thursday, and I often babysat her son. Of course I had no way of knowing that the girl he was going to see was across the street from her.

What are we to do when we see a young suspicious male in a family member's vehicle, anyone?

First we call the family member, right before we call the police, especially if we are a state prison guard.

She called my parents, and they immediately went to get the truck. Calvin went into hiding somewhere. (I don't blame him) He knew my father did not need to get a hold of him at all. While all of that confusion was going on, I began putting on my clothes, but I was interrupted by my mom, who had called with a simple question.

"Where are you?" she asked angrily.

"At target" I said.

All I could think of was why did I just dig myself in deeper. I began conveniently telling her I was at all these random places, thinking that I could stall until Cal came back with the truck. I was completely oblivious to the fact that my parents had the truck the whole time. When my mother told me I had no choice but to tell her where I was. I realized within a few minutes that my daddy had just gotten off from work. It would be bad. Derrick lived around the corner. He wouldn't leave my there alone, though, knowing we both were at fault. The fiasco was ridiculous considering I just plain old knew better. The thing we as teens will do just for a few moments of pleasure is ridiculous. We sat on his mom's beige fluffy couch awaiting my butt whipping. I prayed. It's hilarious, right? All of a sudden, I remembered how to pray.

"Lord I'll except the consequences, just don't let them say I can't see D, and don't let daddy kill him".

That was my prayer, and God blessed me with that much, but I hadn't braced myself for daddy's fury, as much as I thought I had.

I told so many lies that none of them made sense I couldn't remember any of them. Obviously I couldn't drive for months after that.

A couple of days later my daddy out right asked me if my virginity was still intact. I was honest. It hurt to say no sir but I had to. I couldn't lie to them anymore. They took my covenant ring, but at least I had told the truth for once. I didn't deserve it anymore though, every time I looked at it I felt like the biggest hypocrite. I cried out of grief that night, as if someone had died. I thought about every single time my body had been misused, vividly. I thought about everything I had learned about sex from my friends, and every time I heard about how God felt about fornication from spiritual leaders, then the tough part came.

My mother made me call all my spiritual leaders and tell them that I wasn't a virgin anymore. I had to tell my sisters. Their reaction made me want to hang myself. Then she took me to a gynecologist. I was tested for every STD known to man.

That was the doctor's appointment that I found out my reproductive organs were irregular and that I was developing cist. That was the reason why, since eight years old, I have had irregular periods, and horrendous cramps. Sometimes I just didn't get a period for months at a time. My estrogen level was low. All of these things were questioned for a long time, but with one conversation I was given an answer as to why my body formed irregularly.

October 16, 2006 I told my mom and sisters that I had been molested for 6 years and had never said anything. My mom cried, not because of the present moment, she cried because as a child and teen she had also been molested. A lot of times the devil tries to come full circle with his attacks, but God is a healer. We cried for a week every time one of us thought about it.

A week later, Derrick and I were able to see each other again but only on our parents' terms. We had a recommitment meeting between our parents and us, where I received my covenant ring back as a reminder that God forgives us as long as we repent and refrain from recommitting the sin.

After all the fuss and initial shock of me losing my virginity died down, my family (excluding my household) pretty much acted like nothing had happened. However there were certain members who gave me horrible judgment, but I refused to give them the satisfaction of letting them see me cry about it. Some people await the opportunity to ridicule and pass judgment on others simply because they still fill hurt, shame, and guilt from their own past.

CHAPTER NINE

A Brighter Day

From slander to victory I had the fight of my life over the next two years. It was the hardest thing to overcome, to have to be reminded of the past that I had kept hidden, for all of the emotions I had bottled up and avoided letting out, God was causing them to spill out. I didn't know how to react to things that stable human beings would know how to deal with.

My seventeenth year was full of confusion. It was the most blessed, yet tempting year for me thus far. Derrick and I had been through so much dealing with trust issues, and just knowing what was best for each other, that I had fallen deeper into sneaking and lying to my parents to be around him. Oddly Derrick never asked me to do this. I was chasing him to keep him, rather than trusting that he didn't want anyone else but me. He at one time was struggling with staying away from marijuana, and bad influences. That was the one thing that put me over the top with lack of trust in our relationship, simply because from day one I told him I did not want a drug addict, or an alcoholic, nor did I need a jail bird. He knew that. In that situation I didn't judge him. When I finally started trusting him not do any of it anymore, he quit.

We had two big break-ups where I tried to date other people, but no one could be Derrick for me. The only reason why we broke up was because I lost faith and did not want to wait on God to do His work in him. But God joined us together for a reason. It was a connection based on balance. Derrick equals business intelligence, while I equal creative intelligence. Opposites attract, and what balances succeeds, with hard work and fervent prayer.

The wildest part of this ride is how the stress of sin made me sick. I was blacking out, and throwing up, with migraines and horrible stomach aches. I was eventually diagnosed with Polycystic Ovarian Syndrome and Endometriosis. I was developing facial hair, not having periods, but horrible cramps instead and having countless unexplainable days filled with pain. God had to do something, I couldn't live that way. That was God allowing me to finally cry out for help. Healing over all my trauma pain and now sickness was all that I needed to jump start a new life full of anointing and peace and prosperity, but first I had to believe that God WOULD heal me.

I was asked for the third time in my life to stand and tell a testimony. God had issued me a challenge. I needed to sit down, re-evaluate and edit myself before I spoke this time. My first instruction from Him was to open up the session with the statement "I was one of the strongest activists for virginity until marriage, yet I am no longer a virgin". I had to explain why I decided to have sex, and that for the first time in my life I was willing to openly talk about my sexual abuse as a child and the difference between being a child and a teenager going through those things.

As a child you do not understand the severity of the situation. Someone holds you down starts to misuse your body, and when it's over they give you a threatening speech about what they will do to you or what someone else will do to them. When you are a teenager it is a fight, and you fight from beginning to end. You call them horrible names, and you spit at them or you just break down and cry, all because there is nothing else you can do. The older you get you start planning and scheming ways out of a horrible situation in order to rid yourself of this thing that you believe will be the death of you or someone you love.

I had to come to terms with who I used to be, and who I am now, for this group session. When I got there and stood in front of those faces, I knew God was using me for a purpose. After the session a few of the girls got saved, and I was grateful to God for letting me be a part of it.

The adults that attended the session were in complete shock that, I, who was bubbly most of the time, and was so smart, and looked like I had it all together, had been molested for so long. My mother helped me deal with their reactions. I got hugged more than I had ever been hugged by anyone. People cried on my shoulder, because of what I had been through, like they had been their standing along the while watching me be abused, almost like they could vividly depict these terrible moments. I thought it was rather backwards at the time, but it was sympathy and imagination that caused their reactions and eventually I understood. There was some judgment, because obviously my abuse was still no excuse to have sex. I knew that, and as a matter of fact I never said that molestation was my reason for having sex.

I took accountability, and it caused God to show these teens and spiritual leaders to see the leader in me. I was willing from that point on to let God do anything from small to huge in me in order to remain obedient. I wanted that role I wanted to have purpose.

That wasn't my only blessing after restoration. I received a brand new car for my seventeenth birthday. I had some issues with taking it to places it should have not been.

The first day I drove it to school a girl, that didn't like me very much, keyed the bumper. That was the start of a drama filled rest of the year. From February to May 2007 I lost entirely too many friends because of rumors and lies. As Derrick and I grew in God, we slowly fell away from the foolishness we were surrounded by. I personally never missed it and never looked back. It only got better over time. Separation from confusion is the fast track to peace. The sneaking had subsided this year because, I simply wanted better.

CHAPTER TEN

Life's Graduation

When I turned eighteen, I had a very fictitious idea of where I was going in life. I graduated with the belief that I would major in Psychology. That quickly changed to English, then Liberal Arts, then Office Technologies, then Child Care Administration, then finally Deaf Studies. Six majors in one year, now does that sound like a person with any idea what they want to do in life? I think not. Instability means job to job. Everything else, was not working out. I had a poor self-image again. I needed help. I often feel like I wasted a year of my life. I had an extensive resume, with full time qualifications. I wasn't ready for college. I wasn't nearly mature enough, nor was I valuing the information or education. I should've listened to God and used my qualifications to get full-time work until I was honestly ready.

James 1:19-27 (Just listen)

It shocks some Christians that out of everyone they try to confide in, even with billions of other people to watch over, God can still hear one individual's faintest cry.

Presently, even with the weight of adulthood on my shoulders, I can't find one thing to complain about, simply because I recently started giving every worry directly to God. I know God has healed the disease of negativity in my life. As bad as it started off, the extravagance and bliss I'm currently living in cannot be expressed in words. I worked, I gave, I sewed, and I saved all without complaint. It literally feels like Heaven on earth, which blessed me with the revelation that this is how God wants us to feel, whole. God completes me, because He is my creator. The same ways that the components of one parent plus another comes together to create us as humans; God has used that same process with all life. When you sew without complaint, you reap without limitation. The gift I received developed a guide to successful and peaceful living for the rest of my life. God is healer and a restorer.

I have finally, totally, and completely given my whole life to Him. I believe in divine health and healing. He gave me that. There is no more sickness, no more pain, and no more struggling to reach a level that seems absolutely unattainable. I can now walk upright with the truth in the vision that God has set before me.

Over the last two years I have had countless jobs. I've gone from up to down and back so many times. I realized that is because we will send ourselves on a wild goose chase looking for something God has thrown in our faces a million times clearly. It is so sad sometimes. He has an order and plan for all of us. I had to stop and take my assignments given by Him one at a time.

I started by re-evaluating my relationships. My family is amazing. I went back to the basics and apologized to my mom for ever getting beside myself with her. I made a conscious decision to listen to her Godly wisdom from now until forever. Because I admire her so much, I know God will continue to use her to bless and sew into my life with love and guidance. I talked to my sisters and started making a better effort to re-unite trust and love lost because of me losing my virginity. To have a person to look up to one minute, and then in the next you find out that person has totally abandoned a promise they made to you is hard to deal with. I finally got it. I talked to my dad, and all he asked was that I do better and develop my wings. He often used illustrations of what my Grandfather saw in me from birth, because he knew it would strike the right kind of nerve in order for me to do better. It always helped me to grow in every way possible. It seemed as if everything was better than normal at that point, and you know what? It has been ever since.

The next thing I had to re-evaluate was my relationship with Derrick. We had gotten to a place where we had turned our lives around so much that we were viewed as role models for so many young people. In turn we had such a positive image of our relationship. It made us fall deeper in love with the God in each other. Doing right by God had brought so much peace into our lives individually as well as together. On April 17, 2009 he asked me to be his wife. I'll remember it forever. What a journey it was through a year and two months to get to our wedding day. On June 12, 2010, our wedding day, we had the time of our lives, it was awesome. I wanted the man of my dreams and God was just awesome enough to bless me with him. We had a beautiful honeymoon cruise vacation, given to us by my God parents Pastor and Mrs. Carlton J. Sharp.

God made it all possible, the fact that I could be happy, and that this was my truth now. I could be in love, and live a life of peace. At times the past creeps up and tries to grab me, but God uses my husband to console things that hurt and squash the emotions that those images bring. I love that. God gave me that.

Derrick was a gift to me from God that I prayed for. From the time I was ten, I didn't even want to be around boys, but I knew one day God would bless me with the ultimate protector and provider. I saw my parents and wanted the REAL honest young love that they have kept alive even today, after 20 plus years of God given love, faith, and marriage.

D came at a time when nobody else knew the extent of what a blessing he would be except God, not even me. God allowed him to help me begin to value my life, and the people in it. He was able to help me start being me again.

As a man and woman of God, we also get to walk in these callings that He has titled us, and enjoy His presence. We both know our places in ministry now, and it is awesome just to know that God has a place for us. Divine set up, says that we get a chance to use our gifts and God given talents in order to better the Body of Christ and that's all we want.

CHAPTER ELEVEN

Why Write?

Someone once asked me why I write. I told her I used to write to free my mind. Then I woke up. Writing for ventilation, becomes storytelling, telling my story becomes testimony, testimony becomes witness, witness becomes ministry, ministry becomes a lifetime commitment to increasing the body of Christ. Then we become excellent, in turn excellence becomes us.

I am a living testimony. The day I was born I conquered, and the devil has been mad ever since. My mother went through three stages of toxemia, a disease that blocks the blood flow from the mother to the baby. I guess I must've of realized it was killing us both, because I got out of there a month early. That's pretty much how my life was from then on, under grace. To the onlookers obviously it was going to look like I had the perfect childhood. I went to school knowing more than any other kid in my class. My mom is a genius. I was reading by the age of two. I don't know how she did it, but I adore the thought of my intelligence, or the advanced aspects being due to the love a mother has for her children. I was a toddler writing and illustrating my own stories for friends and I to enjoy. I wrote stories depicting my joy for my newborn twin sisters and imaginary friends. The looks of astonishment on people's faces as my parents would present them with the works of art I had created through painting, writing, and drawing, always left me in a confused state. I was surprised that they even cared, much less were impressed. They would take these things that represented my hobbies and things I found fun and treat them like they were masterpieces. The part that I often laughed at was the fact that the older I got people would see so many morals and focuses in these stories and illustrations, than was my intent from the start.

I've been doing this since then, and I don't plan stop until I am unable to do it anymore. Writing the vision and making it plain also means mapping out a plan of obedience. It is God given.

The actual reasons why a lot of people write are for either concrete factual purposes, telling the history of something, to predict, to inform, to entertain, and all of these are good reasons. My very favorite reason is for expression. Any form of expression can manifest to beauty in the little things. Words do impact. Peculiarity and individuality define real people who will never mold or bend to the status quo. I am now the epitome of virtuosity, love, and abundant living. I allowed someone to speak life over me, and believed in the things God was saying through this person. I live in an overflowing fountain of blessings and peace daily. I have to be reminded of that every now and then, but nevertheless it is what it is. God has a covering over my life and the greatest part of this is that satan can't do a thing about it.

Romans 15:18 speaks of not venturing from the word of God. I take that as a personal charge, because that is how I'll remain in this amazing covering, by living totally by the will of God for my life.

We have to seek God about everything in our lives. God is common sense. I am not saying that if you're disobedient that you lack intelligence. The Bible says in Romans 3:23 ALL have sinned and fallen short of the glory of God. Therefore, it's not about your brain. It is about your heart.

Does Jesus dwell there? Obviously I have had my share of screw ups. That's real. It is what you do in order to repent, and find the right way to live, and that's through salvation. Salvation is repenting, and accepting Jesus into your life. It is literally making a choice to make a change. Everything about the way God operates may not make sense to us here, but it absolutely works by faith. He'll give you whatever interpretations and revelations on why He has us to do a thing.

CHAPTER TWELVE

The Heart of a True Believer

The realists of this earth are Godly minded people. People who are described as real always know what to say and how to say it because they are ordained by God to hear what to say and do. They listen to wisdom and instruction for the answers they need. I live in a city so close knit that you could whisper something in Beaumont, Texas and within minutes you have a full blown announcement. If you don't know my family around the city, either you don't read, go to church, or have anything to do with events in the community. Being in such "informative surroundings", I began hiding a great deal of temptation and sin, for my own privacy. Those experiences, realizing the danger in all of them, brought me maturity and understanding. The number one thing they taught me was that most of the time I don't have to open my mouth, and with the strength in my eyes I've said all I need to say. I believe I am here to interpret the words God gives me in my daily life, and write them on paper to minister to others. This is a calling, and as long as I use this gift I am covered. I will forever abide under the shadow of the Almighty.

Psalm 91:1

I want to remain in the heart of God, who knows me even better than my mother, who was the vessel He uses to give me life, who would also die for me, who cares for me. I am here, living, only by the grace of God. In the midst of all of my storms, my faults, or uncontrollable circumstances, His mercy never left me.

I had credible others. These were people my own age who genuinely and sincerely loved me. These three are amazing. God designed us to be there for each other.

First there's Josh Grimes, who is my cousin, but he is also one of my best friends. From day one I have looked up to him. Less than a year older than me, I realize I've spent a lot of time trying to stay on his heels as far as life's experiences. He is another awesome leader I know.

Next is Keisha Sharp, besides hooking me up with the love of my life, she is the person I tell my secrets to first. Whatever reaction she has will always tell me what I'm getting myself into. It sounds funny, but that girl is the truth. We love doing things together. She's my God sister and I love her. Anything we can do with each other always ends up being really fun. We understand each other's pressures and we have so much in common, but that's God with another one of his divine set ups.

The last of this awesome threesome is my Derrick. He taught me to look beyond the surface, let go of my vanity, and just love people. He made me realize that I could not go through life treating people horribly because I had been abused. He gave me kindness, and sincerity, and made it look like something I could do.

These three are amazing; I am honored to have a place in their lives.

The root of my awesomeness is my family. I love them. I have an outstanding mother. I've never seen a woman take on so much from day to day while praising God for everything she comes in contact with during her days. She is the perfect friend, and will tell you the truth in a second. Her elegance, and intellect, and beauty, and overwhelming talent, and spirit filled life style causes me to want to be just like her. My father is the "world's greatest dad". He makes us want to buy every t-shirt, mug, or item that says that quote and shower him with it. He works harder than anyone I know, just to see our family walk in the blessing of God.

I have two sisters. They are twins, Joylann and Jaylann.

Jaylann could possibly be the most compassionate person ever. She's going to make an excellent mother someday. She has a heart of gold. Sometimes I wonder how she can be that sweet. They make straight A's. They have so many awards. I'm so proud of the beautiful young ladies they have become. They constantly amaze me. When I look at them, my little sisters, I see perfection.

Joylann reminds me so much of our mom. She prays, talks, and acts just like her, and I love that. She's got more goals than anyone else I know. I know something else, she'll accomplish every one of them. I tell people all the time that my little sisters are perfect. There's really nothing at all to dislike about them. I love them, flaws, and all. I aspire to take on some of their attributes and characteristics. I seek their wisdom. Brilliance is an understatement to the capacity of their minds, and the things they hold. Book smarts are cool, but my sisters like cultural things and love spiritual things. Joylann has taken up everything from painting, to music, to her chosen career in culinary arts. Jaylann can create, innovate, and design anything set before her. They are going to be the greatest at everything they set their hands to. Habakkuk 2:2.

I believe it's genetic, my parents have owned very successful businesses since before I was born, and I'm the oldest. They were married young. My mom was 19 and my daddy was 21, yet they, with God above all else, were able to create, operate, and maintain a successful business in hair care. My father was blessed to go from working 3 jobs at a time, to moving up through a inner city plant. They've since then branched out into recording studio ministries and youth conferences in surrounding areas. They've even built a studio in our home. God has developed excellence in my parents and he did it so abundantly that people could see the blessed state, just by looking at them. I have a powerful

God, and He made my amazing parents in that particular part of His image.

These people all possess the heart of a true believer.

True believers are often looked at as absent or nonchalant, because of their reactions to certain situations. These are ironically the most brilliant minded people to breathe life's air. If we as prophets and priests of the Body of Christ would just learn to profess that He is now and forever will be the most high, meaning there is NOTHING bigger than God, in every circumstance God will come through every time. In the midst of our humiliation, pain, brokenness, we just have to rejoice. God will show Himself strong. Psalm 68

The heart of a true believer is also a very delicate thing. It is a symbol, showing hurt for people who don't know God's love, and a mission to show them the difference. It is sorrow or grief for the child who dies for lack of knowledge, (Hosea 4:6), tears cried for those perish where there is no vision(Proverbs 29:18). It is a reminder to fight satan with every word that comes out of our mouths. It is an imagination full of visions to better ourselves and others. Lastly it is a joy and peace that surpasses all understanding, whenever we hear the name of Jesus. That is the heart of a true believer.

Philippians 4:7

Even with all of the God minded people surrounding me I still made mistakes. At times I gave satan the upper hand, because I was angry at God. I felt like rather than blaming myself for not telling anyone on my abusers for threatening me that way, I'd blame God for my abuse.

CHAPTER THIRTEEN

The Truth about Deliverance

Once you are truly delivered, you can think about everything from your past, and it will not determine the rest of your day or life. Everything that has happened to me, has given me the drive to do the things God has assigned me to do. I have big dreams, goals, visions, and aspirations. They are God given, so I had to begin to run the race God blessed me with the equipment to run.

Ecclesiastes 2:4-10 talks all about getting on your path, running your race, and not skipping a beat in the process. God made a promise to us that we will have what we say. It's all about speaking life, taking initiative to open our mouths on our own behalves in the Name of Jesus to break chains and bondage in order to live the life of peace and abundance that God has for us.

Also in Ecclesiastes 3: 1-8 He discusses standing firm and maintaining faith because there is a time and a place for everything. Everyone has a season. I personally dealt with a lot through not completely yielding to God, but God had this plan for me and it's now my season.

On October 20, 2006 my journal entry reads as follows:

"Welcome to the wonderful world of a girl who put herself in hell's reach. Have you ever met someone who has completely disowned and disregarded who she was just to taste a small sample of ungodly ground. I was that girl."

I was upset with myself because I had taken the one thing I valued more than anything, my commitment to being a virgin until I was married, and given it away. The worst of this was that once again I had let the abuse I hadn't yet dealt with cause me to do one more thing that I didn't believe in.

I had led some one (Derrick) to believe that it was something I actually wanted to do, when in reality I was giving it before it was taken. It was all I had left, was an actual first time.

They were able to take my first of everything else except that. That is logic to a sexually abused young woman, if at that point logic even exists. This was an act of blatant rebellion, because I felt like God didn't save me from that, so why should I save myself for who He has for me.

In the beginning I did my part. I witnessed to my boyfriend. I gave him Godly wisdom, but I destroyed my witness because I stopped believing in the foundation I was raised on. Even then God kept His hand on me. He showed me grace and mercy constantly.

The definition of MERCY is refraining or cancelling the enforcement of judgment against us. The real reason that He showed me this much mercy at this point was because I knew that Jesus died on the cross for our sins as the ultimate form of showing us mercy. He got rid of judgment for individual sins, and gave us the opportunity to ask for forgiveness, and be completely freed of those sins.

Psalm 118:29 Assures us that God's mercy endures forever. Simply put, it does not stop. God's love for us and His ever revolving grace and mercy, proves that this covering that's on His children is meant to be forever.

After I finally told Derrick about the sexual abuse, he said "no matter what you've been through, you are beautiful, inside and out".

That ignited a heartfelt flame in me. Sex was a sin. Because of that, it took two years of working overtime to present credible others with a positive image of what we stood for as a young CHRISTIAN couple. I had ministered to the youth in so many churches in our community looked up to me and I had accidentally drug Derrick into that light. He grew up with me. God had a plan. Along with writer, singer, author, and public speaker, I have now added wife to the list of my blessed titles, and I love it. God has truly blessed me this year. I am ever evolving into the greatness God has for me, and I love every moment of it.

My husband is the representation of God in my household, and I treat him as such. I am honored to be his helpmate, and God blessed me with a man after His own heart. 1 Samuel 13:13-14

I had chosen to make a bad decision day after day and I subjected myself to real danger. I confessed my sins and God was faithful and just to forgive me of them and cleanse me of all unrighteousness. 1 John 1:9

His mercy purged me of my sins. (Proverbs 16) His forgiveness, and my assurance thereof, was allowing me to live a worry free stress free life all of a sudden. All of my darkness was over and I stepped into the purest light I could've ever imagined. It took some special assignments for God to forgive me. First I had to forgive my molesters. Mark 11:25 Says that in order for God to forgive us we have to forgive our offenders. I forgave them so I could give God my all. In Matthew 23:27 God lays out for us, all the things that unforgiveness can interrupt, including our worship and adoration for Him. That is the reason why worshippers are constantly asked by God to purge, cleanse, and pour out.

Ecclesiastes closes with instructions to obey God and seek Him above all else. This is the foundation to happiness for all believers.

Finally my life is a perfectly written love story on every level. I am in love with the man of my dreams, and he wants to give the world. My parents and I had finally gotten the close relationship that we desired. I can talk to them about ANYTHING. My sisters and I have become best friends. God has become bigger than everything else in my life, and all I had to do was let Him heal and deliver me from the things I lived prisoner to. I can smell peace where ever I set foot. I have become free.

It was a simple concept, once we become disciplined in the things of God we become successful, the opposite of that is if we are not disciplined in the things of God we are unsuccessful, and we will continue to be until the light comes on and we are delivered from a downward spiraling trap.

With God all things are possible. There is NOTHING and NO ONE bigger than Him. In order to get a revelation of that we have to live our lives solely for Him.

There is NO more living life for me, no longer for Jillyann. Now there isn't a doubt in my mind. I can absolutely conquer everything by faith that crosses my path. I know it is far too appropriate to praise God RIGHT NOW. He has showed up, and demanded the blessings he wants for me to come to pass now at the age of twenty, as a newlywed, and a woman of God.

To briefly simplify my whole life's turn around, I have to remind you that I had no life left in me, and now I know, I can speak life with such power, and authority over everything in my life.

With this book I hope I have illustrated that God will do miracles when we accept Him. God blessed me with peace of mind, faith to move mountains, prince charming, and the greatest of all of these is my STORY. When you do things the right way, even when it's your second chance God will give you the ultimate gift. That is your testimony. I am overcome by the blood of the Lamb and the word of my TESTIMONY.

Revelations 12:11

Me in 1992 singing in a program

Me in 1998 at the age of eight

Me in 2004 as a freshman in high school

Me in 2007 before Homecoming

Me on my wedding day
June 12,2 2010

Keisha and I at age 3

Keisha and I at age 12

Keisha and I at age 18

My family and I on Christmas 1999

My family and I singing at the state capital in
Austin, Texas for the 4R Movement on
August 8, 2008

My family and I on my wedding day June 12, 2010

Derrick and I days after we became a
couple in 2006

Derrick and I the week we graduated

Derrick and I on our wedding day June 12, 2010

Derrick and I before his first official sermon
March 7, 2012